Moving from Shattered to Strong

The 12 Steps to Becoming Well

From Sexual Addiction

Matt Burton

Kevin Rose

**Moving from
Shattered to Strong**

THE 12 STEPS TO BECOMING WELL

From Sexual Addiction

**MATT BURTON
KEVIN ROSE**

Copyright © 2024 by Becoming Well, LLC

All rights reserved. No part of this book may be reproduced or transmitted in any form, or by any means, electronic or mechanical, including photocopying, recording, or by information storage or retrieval systems, without permission in writing from the copyright owner.

The views and opinions expressed in this book are those of the author, and do not necessarily reflect the official policy or position of Becoming Well, LLC

Published by Becoming Well, LLC

www.MyBecomingWell.com

Library of Congress Control Number

Paperback ISBN: 979-8-3302-6370-7

E-book ISBN: 979-8-3302-6372-1

Cover design by Monira

Printed in the United States of America

TABLE OF CONTENTS

Step		Page
1	We admitted we were powerless over lust and that our lives had become unmanageable.	1
2	We came to believe that a power greater than ourselves could restore us to sanity.	19
3	We made a decision to turn our will and lives over to the care of our higher power as we understand them.	33
4	We made a searching and fearless moral inventory of ourselves.	47
5	We admitted to our higher power, to ourselves, and to others the exact nature of our wrongs.	63
6	We were entirely ready to have our higher power remove all these defects of character.	73
7	We humbly asked our higher power to remove our shortcomings.	87
8	We made a list of all people we had harmed, and we became willing to make amends to them all.	99
9	We made direct amends to whomever possible, except when to do so would injure them or others.	109
10	We continue to take personal inventory and, when in the wrong, we promptly admit it.	119
11	We seek to improve contact with our higher power through prayer and meditation, praying for knowledge of their will for our lives and the power to carry it out.	137
12	Having had a spiritual awakening from our experience through the steps, we seek to share with others and practice our principles in all our relationships.	147

AUTHORS' NOTE

Although the publisher and the authors have made every effort to ensure that the information in this book was correct at press time and while this publication is designed to provide accurate information regarding the subject matter covered, the publisher and the authors assume no responsibility for errors, inaccuracies, omissions, or any other inconsistencies herein and hereby disclaim any liability to any party for any loss, damage, or disruption caused by errors or omissions, whether such errors or omissions result from negligence, accident, or any other cause.

This publication is meant as a source of valuable information for the reader. However, it is not meant as a substitute for direct expert assistance. If such a level of assistance is required, the services of a competent professional should be sought.

MATT AND LAURA BURTON

www.MyBecomingWell.com

INTRODUCTION

Welcome to the beginning for some and a restart for others of this transformational journey we call recovery. Many come apprehensive, others skeptical. All of us come, if we're truthful, not "all in" with regards to doing whatever it takes to heal our hurts and the hurts we've caused others. One of the puzzle pieces of your recovery includes doing 12-step work.

The original version of the 12 steps was published in 1939 through Alcoholics Anonymous. Though started through A.A., they have since been replicated and used for many different addictions and other destructive coping strategies. From alcohol and drugs, to food and sex, to hoarding, gambling, and work, just to name a few.

We have created our version of both the steps themselves and questions in this workbook to dig deeper in an effort to help you experience and advance your healing in the areas of pornography addiction and sexual addiction, as well as physical and emotionally infidelity.

This step book will guide you methodically through each step as you work through them, either by yourself or - even better - within the context of your connection to a sponsor and recovery group(s). Our hope for you is that you will find transformation both as an individual and within your closest relationships throughout this/your recovery journey.

Other materials available through Becoming Well, LLC and our Becoming Well Intensive Center in Tucson, AZ, may be helpful in your journey and are listed in the appendix of this book with a full list on our website. Virtual sessions for individuals and couples, Recovery Workgroups, Couples Private Intensives, and Guys Group Intensives (Becoming Well Bootcamp), as well as courses, books, and workbooks are also available nationwide and worldwide.

THE 12 STEPS TO BECOMING WELL

Please contact us for further information.

You can visit our website at

www.mybecomingwell.com

for access other resources for you and your partner

Becoming Well, LLC and Becoming Well Intensive Center

Phone number: 520-355-5322

Email address: Info@MyBecomingWell.com

STEP 1

Step 1 - We admitted we were powerless over our lust and that our lives had become unmanageable.

Goals

- Be honest with yourself,
  This is going to feel like a radical shift from how you once lived inside. You are no longer alone, and your struggle is something that you must share with others in order to heal.

- You are not in control.
  You want to begin the practice of letting go of thinking that you have control over how you act in your sexual addiction or other destructive coping strategies. You will discover certain daily practices of surrender, prayer, and boundaries that will help you in the fight against slipping back into destructive patterns.

- Share the burden of recovery.
  We join a recovery group with the hope that we can get help. That help first and foremost comes with making phone calls to others in recovery. The goal is 6/7 calls minimum per week. If needed, call more, whenever you are triggered into acting out. We will and can help each other find a better way to live.

Expectations

- This road of recovery requires routines, boundaries, and daily exercises that take action. Having vision or desire to recover is not enough. Action, or believed behavior, is what your loved ones will see as evidence of your recovery, because action makes your vision of healing become possible.

- Temptations will become less extreme the longer your sobriety lasts. Others in your recovery group will inspire you to press on, get back up, even after a slip. Listen to their guidance and put their feedback into more action.

Hurdles

- Giving up control can feel counterintuitive.
  The 12 steps are built on the understanding that we cannot overcome our struggle with our own willpower, alone.

- You may reach desperation, a thirst, a drive inside you when you begin surrendering over the areas of your life that you need help in. Pride will get in the way.

- Recovery is a marathon, not a race. Take everything one day at a time. Healing for yourself and loved ones will not happen in one day but is progressive, one day at a time.

- Remind yourself that you are worth it, you are worth healing, and you are worth the help others will give you through these desperate times.

Answer the following questions with an honest heart.
Share the answers that impact you the most when working with others in recovery.

"We" is important in this step to acknowledge that you are not alone and the only way to recover is together with support. Recovery is a team sport.

We have been in so many different groups/teams in our life. In what areas of your life have you needed a group in order to be successful? Does it make sense to be in a group in order to be in recovery? Why?

_____
_____
_____
_____
_____
_____
_____
_____
_____
_____

What groups or teams have you played a role in? Describe your roles.

_____
_____
_____
_____
_____
_____
_____

Since stepping into recovery, what does it mean to be a part of a recovery group? What is the value of a recovery group?

_____
_____
_____
_____
_____
_____
_____

Name some challenges you may face when opening up to others for transparency and support.

_____
_____
_____
_____
_____
_____
_____

THE 12 STEPS TO BECOMING WELL

Name the types of groups you currently need in order to fully recover.

_____
_____
_____
_____
_____
_____
_____

What do you need to admit that others know to be true about you?

_____
_____
_____
_____
_____
_____
_____

Name the feelings associated with admitting your struggle to another person.

_____
_____
_____
_____
_____
_____
_____

What has kept you from admitting to yourself the seriousness of your struggle?

_____
_____
_____
_____
_____
_____
_____

Name the specific behaviors or actions you are admitting you are powerless over. List the behaviors and the duration you've had these struggles for.

_____
_____
_____
_____
_____
_____
_____

What consequences in life have led you to believe you are powerless?

_____
_____
_____
_____
_____
_____

"Admitting we are powerless over lust"

This part of Step 1 is crucial. Your addiction and ways of thinking have been formed and rehearsed for many years. Accept it. You're unable to control your sexual acting-out behaviors and way of thinking.

What is the purpose of admitting powerlessness for your recovery?

_____
_____
_____
_____
_____
_____
_____
_____
_____

What do you plan to say to those who will try to diminish or minimize your struggle/addiction?

_____
_____
_____
_____
_____
_____
_____
_____

FROM SEXUAL ADDICTION

Name any evidence that comes to mind that points to a powerlessness over your struggle.

_____
_____
_____
_____
_____
_____
_____

Describe why those reasons above cause powerlessness.

_____
_____
_____
_____
_____
_____
_____

What is the purpose of admitting powerlessness for your recovery?

_____
_____
_____
_____
_____

THE 12 STEPS TO BECOMING WELL

Name 3 feelings you have about being powerless.

1. _____
_____

2. _____
_____

3. _____
_____

Describe the consequences your partner(s) have experienced from your powerlessness.

_____
_____
_____
_____
_____
_____
_____
_____

Thinking about your life in general, what have you experienced that you have had no power over?

_____
_____
_____
_____
_____
_____
_____

FROM SEXUAL ADDICTION

"Our lives have become unmanageable."

You may want to deny this at times, that your life is unmanageable. However, the reality is that you are in recovery for very specific reasons. Owning those reasons is the first step in stepping out of the darkness of denial.

List 5 ways your life has become unmanageable and why.

1. _____
_____

2. _____
_____

3. _____
_____

4. _____
_____

5. _____
_____

What costs has your struggle caused those you care about, besides monetary?

_____
_____
_____
_____
_____
_____

THE 12 STEPS TO BECOMING WELL

Explain why you desire to recover.

_____
_____
_____
_____
_____
_____
_____

In what ways has pain affected your daily life?

_____
_____
_____
_____
_____
_____
_____

Explain the suffering you have endured in your life. Do you feel that your higher power was with you?

_____
_____
_____
_____
_____
_____

Has your pain swayed your belief that your higher power exists?

_____
_____
_____
_____
_____
_____
_____

Hiding can be detrimental to relationships. Name any secrets your family or you have hidden. How were these secrets hidden, and what did they look like?

_____
_____
_____
_____
_____
_____
_____

Name any fears you have that are associated with being honest with yourself and others.

_____
_____
_____
_____
_____
_____

THE 12 STEPS TO BECOMING WELL

In what ways have you tried to avoid taking responsibility and/or being held accountable? Name anything that you have assigned blame to for your actions.

_____
_____
_____
_____
_____
_____
_____

Name fantasies (sexual or otherwise) you have. These can be related to anything other than what your current reality and relationship looks like.

_____
_____
_____
_____
_____
_____
_____

Name how guilt and shame have come out of your sexual addiction.

_____
_____
_____
_____
_____
_____

FROM SEXUAL ADDICTION

How has sexual addiction affected your education?

How have you betrayed your character, morals, and values?

How has your sexual addiction affected your belief system?

THE 12 STEPS TO BECOMING WELL

How has your sexual addiction impacted your finances?

_____
_____
_____
_____
_____
_____

Name any erratic or risky behaviors you have acted on.

_____
_____
_____
_____
_____
_____

Name the destruction your sexual addiction has caused with regards to others and yourself.

_____
_____
_____
_____
_____
_____
_____

FROM SEXUAL ADDICTION

Name the bottom lines that will define if you are "sober" from acting out in your sexual addiction.

Step 1 Summary

List anything you hope to benefit from by completing Step 1.

_____
_____
_____
_____
_____
_____
_____
_____
_____
_____
_____
_____

Have you been honest throughout this step? Why or why not?

_____
_____
_____
_____
_____
_____
_____
_____

Explain why this step sets a foundation for your journey through the steps.

_____
_____
_____
_____
_____
_____
_____

Describe how it has felt to admit powerlessness over your sexual addiction and that your life has become unmanageable.

_____
_____
_____
_____
_____
_____
_____

List what you have learned about yourself during Step 1.

_____
_____
_____
_____
_____
_____

Create a goal that you can set today, and write in a safe place where you will see it, that can help you in your recovery and keep your serenity.

_____
_____
_____
_____
_____
_____
_____
_____
_____
_____
_____
_____
_____
_____
_____
_____
_____
_____
_____
_____
_____
_____
_____
_____

Share your step summary with others in recovery. Be open to their feedback and what they have found in the importance of Step 1.

STEP 2

Step 2 - We came to believe that a power greater than ourselves could restore us to sanity.

Goals

- You begin exploring who your higher power is and has been to you

    - This is a searching and reflection time of recovery. Your history with your higher power is something that needs to be reflected upon.
    - You will share this transformative time in step 2 through daily routines of accepting your feelings, anxieties, and fears in prayer and fellowship throughout your day.
    - Building off of Step 1, there is a desperation for healing you must carry with you throughout recovery. Therefore, a daily choice to believe healing is possible through your higher power is a practice and action that you and you alone must choose.

Expectations

- Daily spiritual practices are essential to recovery

    - AM, PM, and daily surrendering prayers are foundational parts of recovery. Expect to be required to check in with how these practices are going.
    - Share all your heart with your higher power. Bearing your thoughts, feelings, and temptations to your higher power is essential as you emerge from your old habits of hiding.

Hurdles

- **Connecting to your higher power can be mysterious and foreign**

    - **Start with recovery, surrender, and gratitude prayers to your higher power.**
    - **Seek others in recovery for advice and help with where to start. Remember it is one day at a time, one prayer at a time, and one choice at a time.**
    - **Prayer can feel awkward and shameful following the weight of relationship destruction. Remember that your higher power hears you and wants healing for you. Your higher power doesn't want the addictions that brought you into recovery to be the end of your story. Your higher power wants you to live a life of health and have a victorious ending to your story.**

Answer the following questions with an honest heart.
Share the answers that impact you the most with others in recovery.

Name the areas of your life that have lost sanity. Insanity is doing the same thing over and over again and expecting different results. Share them with a group member this week.

_____
_____
_____
_____
_____
_____
_____
_____
_____
_____
_____
_____
_____

FROM SEXUAL ADDICTION

Describe what it would look like to be free from the above behaviors, and to change.

___

Name any boundaries you have broken while acting out in your sexual addiction.

___

We say each week that we are 100% responsible for our actions in our life. Do you believe that? Who do you tend to place blame on?

THE 12 STEPS TO BECOMING WELL

Name 5 traits of your higher power.

1. _____
   _____

2. _____
   _____

3. _____
   _____

4. _____
   _____

5. _____
   _____

Of those 5, are any of them new to you?

_____
_____
_____
_____
_____
_____
_____
_____
_____
_____
_____

Describe how your belief in a higher power has affected your sexual addiction in the past and present.

_____
_____
_____
_____
_____
_____
_____

Describe your relationship with your higher power. Name anything that has led you away from belief in your higher power.

_____
_____
_____
_____
_____
_____
_____

Describe a spiritual experience you've had or would like to have.

_____
_____
_____
_____
_____

Describe how you have been defiant and/or strayed away from relying upon a higher power.

_____
_____
_____
_____
_____
_____

Name 3 recovery tools that have been helping you recover thus far. Explain why you believe they are helpful.

1. _____
_____
_____

2. _____
_____
_____

3. _____
_____
_____

What has someone shared that worked for them, which you are willing to apply in your own life?

_____
_____
_____
_____
_____

Now, describe a specific tool someone else has used to build trust that you are willing to actively apply in your own relationships.

_____
_____
_____
_____
_____
_____
_____

Describe your experience with your high power's presence in your life. Name 3 daily habits that have cultivated the possibility of those experiences.

_____
_____
_____
_____
_____
_____
_____
_____

1. _____
   _____
2. _____
   _____
3. _____
   _____

THE 12 STEPS TO BECOMING WELL

How can your higher power help you recover? Describe your belief about their impact on your recovery.

_____
_____
_____
_____
_____
_____
_____

List areas of your life that can be restored with the aid of your higher power. What will it look like to be restored in each area?

_____
_____
_____
_____
_____
_____
_____

In the areas listed above, how has your higher power already been providing restoration?

_____
_____
_____
_____
_____
_____
_____

For your sanity, name 3 areas within your sexual addiction that you need your higher power to bring restoration to.

1. _____
   _____
   _____

2. _____
   _____
   _____

3. _____
   _____
   _____

For the 3 you named above, provide behaviors someone will see in you that will provide evidence of your restoration.

_____
_____
_____
_____
_____
_____
_____

How have your views of your higher power changed over time?

_____
_____
_____
_____
_____

Name individuals who have influenced your attitude towards your higher power. Share how each of them influenced you.

_____
_____
_____
_____
_____
_____
_____

With regards to your upbringing, what obstacles do you face in trusting your higher power?

_____
_____
_____
_____
_____
_____
_____

Now, name any strengths your upbringing has given you.

_____
_____
_____
_____
_____
_____

Describe how your higher power is working in your life right now.

_____
_____
_____
_____
_____
_____
_____
_____
_____
_____
_____
_____

How did your family of origin view the act of asking for help from others?

_____
_____
_____
_____
_____
_____
_____
_____
_____
_____

List 3 questions or doubts about the existence of your higher power. Share these questions with others in recovery. Ask someone in recovery to answer these questions and record their answers here.

1. _____
   _____
   _____

2. _____
   _____
   _____

3. _____
   _____
   _____

Step 2 Summary

Congratulations on completing your second step.

Now, write a summary of what you have learned about yourself in the space below.

Include:

- **What you have learned about yourself,**
- **your sexual addiction, and**
- **what you must choose to do in order to stay in recovery.**

Describe how **Step 2** has been a choice to believe in the help that a higher power can give to us.

_____
_____
_____
_____
_____
_____
_____
_____
_____
_____
_____
_____
_____
_____
_____
_____

THE 12 STEPS TO BECOMING WELL

Share your step summary with others in recovery. Be open to their feedback and what they have found in the importance of Step 2.

STEP 3

Step 3 - We made a decision to turn our will and lives over to the care of our higher power as we understand them.

Goals

- This is a decision, not made in one day or in one minute, but every day, every prayer, and every phone-call cry for help as we live a different life from the one we lived before.
- We need to make and revise boundaries to keep us sober in our recovery whenever triggering situations arise.
- We live in fellowship, turning over our lives to our higher power. This will involve honest assessment of the areas in our lives that may be unhealthy.

Expectations

- **Freedom is found in full surrender.**
  - Our weaknesses are where we begin turning over lives over in order to receive healing and newfound strength.
  - This is when we get into the details of where we need to turn over control. Whatever way you act out sexually, you will need to examine anything and everything that you idolize and obsess over that takes the place of your higher power in your heart.
  - Sharing any anxiety or hesitation with those further in recovery than you will aid you in step 3.

Hurdles

- Turning over our lives could mean changing where we spend our time, money, and attention. The truths your higher power will begin revealing to you about unhealthy habits, relationships, and entertainments can be hard to accept.

- Trusting in your higher power is easier said than done. This is a daily practice, and if done with honesty and submission, it will be a painful and rewarding battle won with your higher power by your side.

- Moving on without fully submitting your life and will implies you aren't ready to move into Step 4. So slow down. One day at a time, seek your higher power in prayer and turn to others for help. Remember, you are worth it!

Answer the following questions with an honest heart.
Share the answers that impact you the most with others in recovery.

Name the rock bottoms that have brought you to a point of desperation to turn your will over to your higher power.

_____
_____
_____
_____
_____
_____
_____
_____
_____
_____
_____
_____
_____
_____

List all the struggles and addictions you are choosing to surrender your own power and will over.

_____
_____
_____
_____
_____
_____
_____

Describe when and why you made a choice to turn your life and will over to your higher power in the past.

_____
_____
_____
_____
_____
_____
_____

Describe what desperation means in regard to your recovery.

_____
_____
_____
_____
_____
_____

In reflection of times when you've felt desperate for recovery in the past, how is this moment in time different? Why?

_____
_____
_____
_____
_____
_____
_____

What changes are you beginning to experience as a result of turning your life and will over to your higher power?

_____
_____
_____
_____
_____
_____
_____

What moments or events coalesced into this decision to turn your life and will over to your higher power for recovery?

_____
_____
_____
_____
_____
_____

List the areas in your life for which you are hesitant to give control to your higher power. Identify feelings for each.

_____
_____
_____
_____
_____
_____
_____

What steps will you take to surrender control over the areas listed above to your higher power?

_____
_____
_____
_____
_____
_____
_____

List daily habits you are currently implementing in order to give over your will.

_____
_____
_____
_____
_____
_____

THE 12 STEPS TO BECOMING WELL

Name evidence of your higher power's care for you, which you have seen since turning turned your life over to your higher power.

_____
_____
_____
_____
_____
_____
_____
_____
_____
_____
_____
_____
_____

Which areas of your life are you willing to have your higher power take authority over?

_____
_____
_____
_____
_____
_____
_____
_____
_____

Exercise:

Contact 3 people from recovery in the next 2 weeks. Ask them about what it looked like for them to turn their will over to their higher power, along with the areas that may have been challenging at first to surrender control over.

Person #1: _____

What they said:

_____
_____
_____
_____
_____
_____
_____
_____

Person #2: _____

What they said:

_____
_____
_____
_____
_____
_____
_____
_____

Person #3: _____

What they said:

_____
_____
_____
_____
_____
_____
_____
_____
_____

Use the feelings wheel to list specific feelings you are having related to trusting your higher power with your life (see appendix).

_____
_____
_____
_____
_____
_____
_____
_____

FROM SEXUAL ADDICTION

Name the ways you have tried to control and make up for your addictions on your own.

_____
_____
_____
_____
_____
_____
_____

Name the frustrations and doubts you hold about yourself and your higher power.

_____
_____
_____
_____
_____
_____
_____

Aside from the struggles/addictions that brought you into recovery, have there been any revelations about additional struggles in your life?

_____
_____
_____
_____
_____
_____

Our caregivers set an example for how we begin viewing our higher power in our lives. List relationships in your life in which someone was supposed to care for you but didn't. How did those relationships impact your views of your higher power?

_____
_____
_____
_____
_____
_____

Do you typically see others as being better or worse than you? How does your higher power view you?

_____
_____
_____
_____
_____
_____

Describe how you have typically measured yourself as good or bad.

_____
_____
_____
_____
_____
_____

Describe any doubts you have about your higher power accepting you. Name anything you have done that has created that doubt.

_____
_____
_____
_____
_____
_____
_____
_____
_____
_____
_____
_____

How are you working towards opening up to others in recovery on a regular basis?

_____
_____
_____
_____
_____
_____
_____
_____
_____

Exercise:

There are red light behaviors, yellow light behaviors, and green light behaviors.

- **Red light actions are when you act out.**
- **Yellow light actions are on the edge, not completely acting out but heading towards acting out.**
- **Green lights are safe actions.**

Create your Red, Yellow, and Green light list.

Red:

_____
_____
_____
_____
_____
_____
_____
_____
_____

Yellow:

_____
_____
_____
_____
_____
_____
_____
_____

Green:

Step 3 Summary

Congratulations on completing your third step.

Now, write a summary of what you have learned about yourself in the space below.

Include:

- What you have learned about yourself,
- your addiction, and
- what you must choose in order to rely upon your higher power's will and power in your life.

Describe how **Step 3** has been a choice to believe in the help that a higher power can give to us.

_____
_____
_____
_____
_____
_____
_____
_____
_____
_____
_____
_____
_____
_____
_____

FROM SEXUAL ADDICTION

___

Share your step summary with others in recovery. Be open to their feedback and what they have found in the importance of Step 3.

STEP 4

Step 4 - We made a searching and fearless moral inventory of ourselves.

Goals

- This is where honesty gets put into action. We document and reflect on our past in:
  - Sexual history and Infidelity harms done to us
  - Sexual history and Infidelity harms done to others

We reflect upon how we acted out, why we acted out, and the feelings that we associate with the actions that we committed or that were done to us.

Expectations

- By listing out our history, we begin searching for full honesty with our higher power and others.
- We may need to add to our inventory as time passes.
- It is not necessary to disclose your inventory. Talking to a recovery coach, a therapist, or trusted spiritual leader will create a safe space to vent feelings associated with revisiting the past.
- Disclosure in a marriage may be necessary, BUT be sure to create plans for such a disclosure with appropriate planning and guidance, using individual and couples recovery counseling or coaching.
- Becoming Well providers are an option for help with this process. We can create a safe space for such a disclosure to be accomplished with the least amount of pain possible
- We have experience and are certified and trained, but we also know firsthand from our own history of recovery, that disclosure can look many different ways for different couples. The key is to be honest to the extent that it will help your partner feel safe.

Hurdles

- Emotions are raw when listing out your history of destruction from your sexual addiction and other tendencies. At this point, leaning on your higher power and recovery partners will be essential to overcome the inevitable grief you will feel while recording your inventory.

  - Have a list of people to call handy whenever you're working through your inventory.

- You may feel broken and not worthy of healing while listing out the pain you have caused others.

  - Return to the foundation of Steps 1, 2, and 3, and remind yourself that your higher power wants nothing less than to free you from your addictions.

- Adjust your daily recovery prayers to grieve the pain and seek your higher power for the strength to live a life in full surrender.
- Seek others in recovery who have experienced the freedom from completing a thorough Step 4 inventory. This step can and should be thorough. Take your time, because it will be worth the effort.

Answer the following questions with an honest heart.
Share the answers that impact you the most with others in recovery.

Sexual Acting Out/Acting In Inventory

Filling out your Sexual Inventory history will be your first step in identifying and bringing to the light the actions you have done and that others have done toward you. Use the questions below to help guide you in filling out your inventory.

Who have you acted out sexually with?	When was your first sexual experience?	Have you experienced anything happening sexually towards you without your permission?
Have you had sexual secrets?	Have you ever been sexually abused?	Have you been exposed to pornographic material without your consent?

***More questions pertaining to your sexual history can be found in the *Sexaholics Anonymous White Book*. Use this or other resources to completely flesh out your sexual history in terms of **sexual acting out and acting in, harms done to others, and harms done to us.**

Use the tables on the following page to:

- **list the people, places, or groups in your sexual history,**
- **what happened (the story),**
- **your reaction (your actions or inactions),**
- **and the reason you acted out (nature/feeling associated to your behaviors)**

Use support from your workgroup partners and facilitator as a resource to aid in your inventory.

THE 12 STEPS TO BECOMING WELL

Sexual Acting Out/Acting In History – Harms Done to Me (Fill out ONLY if you have experienced sexual abuse, harm, exposure to explicit material, and/or other sexual traumas)

Subject	What Happened	My Reaction (Door A)	My Reason
Sexual history with:_____ *List the people, places, or groups*	The situation or circumstance tied to sexual behavior: _____ *Tell the story(ies) of when you would act out sexually*	The behaviors I took were_____ *Describe your feelings and behaviors*	I acted the way I did out of_____ *Name the nature of your reasons (ex: fear, selfishness, loneliness, prideful, control, comfort...)*

Sexual Acting Out/Acting In History – Harms Done to Others

Subject	What Happened	My Reaction (Door A)	My Reason
Sexual history with:_____ *List the people, places, or groups*	The situation or circumstance tied to sexual behavior: _____ *Tell the story(ies) of when you would act out sexually*	The behaviors I took were_____ *Describe your feelings and behaviors*	I acted the way I did out of_____ *Name the nature of your reasons (ex: fear, selfishness, loneliness, prideful, control, comfort...)*

Step 4 Summary

Congratulations on completing your fourth step.

● Now, write a summary of what you have learned about yourself in the space below. **Include:**

- **What parts of your inventory were hardest/easiest to reflect on?**
- **Patterns in your SA acting-out**
- **Specific "Natures" you tend to resort to in SA (last column)**

FROM SEXUAL ADDICTION

Share your step summary with others in recovery. Be open to their feedback and what they have found in the importance of Step 4.

FROM SEXUAL ADDICTION

STEP 5

Step 5 - We admitted to our higher power, to ourselves, and to others the exact nature of our wrongs.

Goals

- This is where you become fully vulnerable, an open book, about your history to your higher power and to others.

  - You will share your inventory with a recovery partner.
  - Disclosure to your significant other may be overdue and needed, so you will need to seek help in how to give a full disclosure. Becoming Well can help with that, or any other trained recovery coach or counselor who specializes in disclosure delivery.

- Admitting to your higher power is an ongoing process. Accepting the nature of your wrongs is an intimate process that starts with daily honesty with your higher power.
- Aim to fit time into your daily prayers and recovery work to speak light to your inventory, sharing it with your higher power.

Expectations

- Sharing your story will be freeing and uplifting. You will see a huge stride in momentum in your recovery during this step.

  - Keeping this momentum is important to be able to complete the 12-step process.

- The peace you feel from being open and honest, for maybe the first time ever, can be an exciting rush.

  - Therefore, that freedom is very personal. Others may not be feeling the freedom you are. Remaining under the pain they may still be experiencing is expected.

- Whatever it is that you may have said to yourself, "I will take this to my grave" is exactly what you need to share with another and confess to your higher power. Your healing and recovery depend on it.

Hurdles

- Fear and secrecy can get in the way of being vulnerable and honest. The lies that your pain and addiction will tell you can get in the way of your recovery and healing.
- As mentioned before, your freedom and relief in being completely honest may be viewed negatively by loved ones, especially any you have betrayed.
  - Be prepared to use tools to give space for their feelings of pain that persist or flare up. It is understandable for them to still feel pain.
  - If you need help understanding the other person's feelings, consult with a Becoming Well provider or other trained professionals.
- Always, always remember: you are worth recovery.

Answer the following questions with an honest heart.
Share the answers that impact you the most with others in recovery.

List any reasons why it is difficult to admit your wrongs. Share your reasons with others in recovery that have completed their Step 5.

_____
_____
_____
_____
_____
_____
_____
_____
_____

List the most memorable times in your past when you wronged another with your behavior.

_____
_____
_____
_____
_____
_____
_____

When you share your inventory with another, what expectations do you have of them?

_____
_____
_____
_____
_____
_____
_____

Contact your recovery partner and schedule a time to share your inventory with them. Write the name of the person and the date and time you have scheduled to complete this.

_____
_____
_____
_____
_____

After sharing with your Step 5 recovery partner, is there anything you didn't share about? If so, list the items you have not shared from your inventory and prepare to disclose them to your recovery partner as soon as possible. Being honest and open about your past is essential to your healing and recovery.

_____
_____
_____
_____
_____
_____

Describe your experience and feelings about admitting your wrongs to another.

_____
_____
_____
_____
_____
_____

What have you learned about yourself through the process of telling your story to another?

_____
_____
_____
_____
_____

List the most meaningful exercises, practices, and experiences you have had in recovery thus far.

_____
_____
_____
_____
_____
_____
_____

List the challenging parts of recovery for you thus far.

_____
_____
_____
_____
_____
_____

Would your family consider you to be humble? Why or why not?

_____
_____
_____
_____
_____
_____

List the standards of living that allowed you to keep your addiction in secret and that enabled it to survive.

_____
_____
_____
_____
_____
_____

Name the feelings you have that keep you from being honest with yourself and others. Share these with a recovery partner.

_____
_____
_____
_____
_____
_____

Are you fearful, ignorant, or prideful about sharing your struggles in recovery? If so, explain the reasons for each.

_____
_____
_____
_____
_____
_____
_____

List specific patterns of lies from your inventory that have kept you isolated in your addiction.

_____
_____
_____
_____
_____
_____
_____

After sharing with your recovery partner, list what you have learned regarding fear, trust, and acceptance.

_____
_____
_____
_____
_____
_____
_____

Name any differences between sharing your struggle with a person and with your higher power.

_____
_____
_____
_____
_____
_____

What will you plan on doing if you forget to share something in your inventory with your recovery partner?

_____
_____
_____
_____
_____
_____
_____
_____

Step 5 Summary

Congratulations on completing your fifth step.

- **Now, write a summary of what you have learned about yourself in the space below. Include:**
  - **What parts of your inventory were hardest/easiest to reflect on**
  - **Patterns in your SA acting out**
  - **Specific "Natures" you tend to resort to in SA (last column)**

_____
_____
_____
_____
_____
_____
_____
_____
_____
_____
_____
_____
_____
_____
_____
_____
_____
_____

Share your step summary with others in recovery. Be open to their feedback and what they have found in the importance of Step 5.

STEP 6

Step 6 - We were entirely ready to have our higher power remove all these defects of character.

Goals

- Here's where we become ready for change.
  - It may include giving up habits, attitudes, or ways of thinking.
  - Whatever the defect is, that you identified in your inventory, your target in this step is to prepare your heart for putting those behaviors and addictions behind you.
- Be open for criticism and reflection.
  - If your actions are still a reflection of your defects, then you will need to be open to humility.
  - In this process, you may need to add to and record an ongoing inventory.

Expectations

- This step will consolidate and summarize the defects you identified from your inventory.
- You will need to share this process of summing up your flaws with others in recovery.
- Healing involves simply saying out loud that you are ready. Pray regularly, AM, PM, and throughout the day to prepare for your higher power to help you remove your character defects.

Hurdles

- Being ready for defects to be removed, may involve removing unhealthy habits, pastimes, or relationships from your life.
    - Help from others in recovery and your higher power will reveal aspects of your life that need to be removed.
    - Removing your defects can be painful, like going into surgery. Exercises like appreciation and resignation letters can help with letting things go from your past.
- Seek guidance from others in recovery and hear how they became ready for their higher power to remove their character defects.
- Keeping true to daily submission, this is a one-day-at-a-time process, so let go and let your higher power and others help you prepare to begin moving past your character defects and into a new life.

Answer the following questions with an honest heart.
Share the answers that impact you the most with others in recovery.

List events in your life where you were motivated to act and change.

_____
_____
_____
_____
_____
_____
_____
_____
_____
_____
_____
_____

Describe your higher power's role in your recovery thus far through Steps 1-5 in a short paragraph. Include your feelings, habits, and relationship towards your higher power. Also, include why you believe you have needed your higher power throughout the recovery process.

_____
_____
_____
_____
_____
_____
_____
_____
_____
_____
_____

If your struggles and character defects were removed, what feelings would you have?

_____
_____
_____
_____
_____
_____
_____
_____

List out the character defects you have identified from inventory (Step 4) in regards to your addiction. Then, write a short paragraph explaining what life would be like without them and what life would be like if you continued acting out in them.

Defect	Paragraph

Name anything you are unwilling to do or change in order to gain freedom from your addiction.

_____
_____
_____
_____
_____
_____

Name any desires, passions, pleasures, or loves that you are not yet ready to turn away from.

_____
_____
_____
_____
_____
_____

Reflect on any behavior patterns or coping mechanisms from your Step 4 inventory and list out some people, places, or decisions that tend to lead you toward those behaviors.

_____
_____
_____
_____
_____
_____

What decisions can you make today to turn away from your addiction?

_____
_____
_____
_____
_____
_____
_____
_____
_____

Name any desires you fear will not be satisfied if you turn them over to your higher power.

_____
_____
_____
_____
_____
_____
_____

Describe what life would be like if your addiction no longer directed you in response to hardship and conflict.

_____
_____
_____
_____
_____
_____

Name the changes you need to make that you know are or will be the most difficult in your recovery.

_____
_____
_____
_____
_____
_____
_____

List any desires that your higher power has already begun changing.

_____
_____
_____
_____
_____
_____
_____

Then, list any new desires since joining recovery.

_____
_____
_____
_____
_____
_____

List any old patterns and ways you have already begun turning from.

_____
_____
_____
_____
_____
_____

Then, name new habits and practices you are developing.

_____
_____
_____
_____
_____
_____

Name any relationships that need to change in your life in order for you to recover. Specify the ones that need to end, change, or continue to grow.

_____
_____
_____
_____
_____
_____

Willing and Help Needed Exercise:

Left Column: List out the specific character defects you are currently willing to turn over to your higher power. Pray over each one this week and share them with a recovery partner.

Right Column: List out the character defects you need help letting go of. Pray over these on your own and with a recovery partner, asking specifically for your higher power's help to turn them over.

Character Defects I am Willing to Turn Over to **my Higher Power**	Defects I Need to Help Turning Over to **my Higher Power**

Affirmations Exercise:

Name a self-affirmation about your character every day for the next 7 days.

Being able to recognize and see the new you in recovery brings confidence and a new identity. Then, write a prayer of gratitude for these characteristics you see in yourself.

Day	Self-Affirmation	Prayer of Gratitude
1		
2		
3		
4		
5		
6		
7		

Step 6 Summary

Congratulations on completing your sixth step.

- **Now, write a summary of what you have learned about yourself in the space below. Include:**

    - **What character defects are you willing to have your higher power remove?**
    - **What areas of your life need to change for their removal?**
    - **What self-affirmation(s) comforted you about who your higher power has created you to be?**

_____
_____
_____
_____
_____
_____
_____
_____
_____
_____
_____
_____
_____
_____
_____
_____
_____
_____
_____
_____

THE 12 STEPS TO BECOMING WELL

Share your step summary with others in recovery. Be open to their feedback and what they have found in the importance of Step 6.

STEP 7

Step 7 - We humbly asked our higher power to remove our shortcomings.

Goals

- This is a process of practicing full surrender.
  - Create prayers to your higher power asking them to remove your character defects.
  - Imagine what life would be like without your struggle or addiction
- Ongoing Inventory needs to be taken daily
  - When a defect arises, return to asking your higher power for its removal

Expectations

- Full recovery involves sharing your struggles with others. This is a key way to involve others and your higher power in the process of removal.
- A key to success is:
  - Trusting fully in your higher power.
  - Believing that your higher power can help.
- Strong emotion may rush out when you're imagining the removal of your defect.
- The feeling of desperation is good.
- Thirsting for a new way of living, provided by your higher power, is a gift.

Hurdles

- **This is the place where you've passed the halfway mark through the 12 steps, so don't give up!**
- **Half efforts now will yield half results later.**
- **Practicing forgiving yourself, one defect at a time, and asking for their removal one at a time is how you begin to love yourself and in turn become able to love others fully.**

Answer the following questions with an honest heart.
Share the answers that impact you the most with others in recovery.

List out experiences in which you have displayed humility.

_____
_____
_____
_____
_____
_____
_____
_____
_____
_____
_____
_____
_____
_____
_____
_____
_____
_____
_____

Name the feelings you had when you displayed a humble attitude.

_____
_____
_____
_____
_____
_____
_____

Name anything that you have asked your higher power for and in turn received.

_____
_____
_____
_____
_____
_____
_____
_____
_____
_____

Reflect upon your character defects from Step 6 and list out the ones you would like to ask your higher power to remove.

_____
_____
_____
_____
_____
_____
_____

Describe your higher power's character as you ask for your defects to be removed. If you have experienced those characteristics from your higher power in the past, describe how.

What are your expectations when asking things of your higher power?

Ask 3 others in recovery who have gone through Step 7 and record their experiences here.

Person #1: _____

What they said:

_____
_____
_____
_____
_____
_____
_____
_____
_____
_____

Person #2: _____

What they said:

_____
_____
_____
_____
_____
_____
_____
_____
_____
_____

Person #3: _____

What they said:

_____
_____
_____
_____
_____
_____
_____

Use the feelings wheel to list specific feelings you are having in relation to trusting your higher power.

_____
_____
_____
_____
_____
_____
_____
_____
_____
_____
_____
_____

List out each character defect from Step 6 below.

Then, next to each, write a prayer to your higher power asking for their removal.

Pray for strength to surrender the defects over, giving your higher power control over them, and the wisdom to make healthy decisions to move towards recovery.

Give your higher power a sense of prioritization over which is to be removed first, and then honestly rank them in their order of importance and urgency. This process may take days. If you don't see a clear ranking, continue to pray over them and bring up the struggle to a recovery partner.

Be prepared to share the top 2 prayers you have written in your Step Summary.

Defect	Prayer

THE 12 STEPS TO BECOMING WELL

Name ways you have tried to change on your own with no success.

_____
_____
_____
_____
_____
_____
_____

Write a personal mission statement for your life from this day forward.

_____
_____
_____
_____
_____
_____
_____

Would you be satisfied if your higher power removed the defect(s) that brought you to recovery? Why or why not?

_____
_____
_____
_____
_____
_____
_____

Name 2 actions you can take to strengthen your relationship with your higher power.

1. _____

2. _____

Exercise: Name actions in daily, weekly, and monthly practices that you are taking to become:	
Honest	
Selfless	
Considerate	
Courageous	

Step 7 Summary

Congratulations on completing your seventh step.

- **Now, write a summary of what you have learned about yourself in the space below. Include:**

  - **Two prayers from the exercise above and describe your feelings while putting them into practice.**
  - **Any fears or feelings associated with your higher power removing your defects.**

_____
_____
_____
_____
_____
_____
_____
_____
_____
_____
_____
_____
_____
_____
_____
_____
_____
_____
_____
_____
_____

Share your step summary with others in recovery. Be open to their feedback and what they have found in the importance of Step 7.

STEP 8

Step 8 - We made a list of all people we had harmed, and we became willing to make amends to them all.

Goals

- Reflect on the people and organizations you wronged from your inventory.
- If you think of someone or some group you have missed, list them out as well in this step.
- Become clear on what making amends is and what it isn't.
- Have multiple discussions with those who have completed amends before. Take notes on how it went for them.
- Become willing by your higher power's strength, not your own. Surrender personal judgements and seek to forgive prior to entering an amends.

Expectations

- Amends Is NOT…
  - Expecting forgiveness from the person you harmed.
  - About sharing reasons for your addictions.
  - Placing blame for your addiction on traumas you've endured.
  - Expecting the other party to own their wrongs.
- Amends Is…
  - Communicating your faults and taking responsibility.
  - Recognizing the pain you have caused.
  - Asking for forgiveness.
- Becoming willing is another process involving prayer.
- Forgiving others for their wrongs frees you to be able to love them from this day on, whether they want to reconcile a relationship with you or not.

Hurdles

- **Feelings can get in the way of making your amends**

  - **Anger, resentment, pride, malice... basically anything that breeds a defensive or entitled stance**
  - **Unforgiveness is at the root of your judgment towards someone. Forgiving them says, "I am handing their judgment over to your higher power who is just."**

- **Becoming willing to make amends can look different depending on if a face-to-face amends will harm someone. Being willing to give a face-to-face amends is best, but Step 9 will explore other options.**
- **Owning up to your role in causing others pain can be frightening. Asking your higher power for the courage you need can be added to your daily prayers. Discuss such hesitancies with someone in recovery. Remember, you are worth it to your higher power and your loved ones to own your mistakes.**

Answer the following questions with an honest heart.
Share the answers that impact you the most with others in recovery.

Reflect upon your progress in recovery and the 12-Step process.

In Steps 1-3 you admitted your need for a higher power and have placed your trust in that belief.

Then, in Step 4, you created an inventory of all the harms you have done and suffered from others.

Most recently, in Steps 5-7, you identified the nature of your wrongs and asked your higher power for the removal of your defects.

Now you must reflect on those in your inventory whom you have harmed and become willing to make amends to them. It is only now, in the progress of your recovery, that you are capable of recognizing the pain and harm you have caused in complete detail and honesty.

List out the people, places, and organizations you have wronged in the first column.

In the second column, name the pain in general that you have caused.

People, places, and organizations	Pain, wrong, or betrayal caused

Continued	
People, places, and organizations	Pain, wrong, or betrayal caused

Name the primary feelings you felt while making your list.

_____
_____
_____
_____
_____
_____

In becoming willing to make amends, we must understand what amends is and isn't.

Amends is/isn't:

- Is taking responsibility for your role you've played
- Is not others' responsibilities
- Is identifying the hurt you've caused another
- Is not denying or excusing the hurt others have caused you
- Should not be avoided if someone is unaware of your activity
- Does not free you from potential consequences for your actions
- Is doing your part to repair your wrongs in the relationship, whether or not others take ownership of their own needs for recovery
- Is not reconciliation
- Is not necessarily done face-to-face when an amends may hurt another

False Motives – the purpose of making your amends is:

- Not to draw out an amends from another
- Not to make someone like or accept you
- Not to be heard or express your own hurt
- Not to hurt another out of demonstrating your perspective or defense
- Not to punish or shame yourself

Describe in your own words what it would look like to be willing to make amends to another.

List out the names of people, places, or organizations you are willing/not willing to make amends with and why for each.

Then, write a prayer for strength through a will other than your own (Step 3 principle) to help you become willing to make amends.

Write a prayer for each person in your list whom you're hesitant to make amends with. Share this prayer with someone in recovery who has done Steps 8 and 9.

Then, record their contact information once you become willing to make amends.

Note: It is understandable to be hesitant in Step 8 for a time in order to become willing to make amends.

People, places, and organizations	Why not willing	Prayer and Contact Information

THE 12 STEPS TO BECOMING WELL

Describe your struggle with guilt and shame related to your sexual acting-out related behaviors.

_____
_____
_____
_____
_____
_____
_____

Who have you falsely blamed? List them and explain.

_____
_____
_____
_____
_____
_____

What exercises or daily practices have you obtained in recovery that can help you accept yourself for the harms you have done to others and yourself?

_____
_____
_____
_____
_____
_____

Step 8 Summary

Congratulations on completing your eighth step.

- **Now, write a summary of what you have learned about yourself in the space below. Include:**
  - **Explain what amends is and isn't in your own words.**
  - **Name any person, place, or organization you are not yet willing to make amends with and your reason why.**

_____
_____
_____
_____
_____
_____
_____
_____
_____
_____
_____
_____
_____
_____
_____
_____
_____
_____
_____
_____

THE 12 STEPS TO BECOMING WELL

Share your step summary with others in recovery. Be open to their feedback and what they have found in the importance of Step 8.

STEP 9

Step 9 - We made direct amends to whomever possible, except when to do so would injure them or others.

Goals

- Decide who you can deliver an amends face-to-face to.
  - This will be a hard decision and will depend on whether or not giving a face-to-face amends will harm the person you have wronged and whether or not they will want to receive your amends.
  - Counsel from others who have given their amends before is essential.
- Write amends to every person or group from your inventory whom you have harmed. This is a healing process for you.
- You will need to read your rough drafts to someone experienced in giving amends and make revisions.
- And finally, give your amends.

Expectations

- So here it is, a recipe for amends letter writing, RUT-ABC
  - R - Recognize the Wrong
  - U - Understanding the Hurt
  - T - Take Responsibility
  - A - Ask for Forgiveness
  - BC - Behavior Change
- You will use your inventory to direct much of this process. There is a lot of explanation for what Amends is, what it isn't, and what each part of RUT-ABC should look like.

- This process can take a substantial amount of time. It is understandable. Practice delivering the amends that are more challenging and prepare for the possible feelings the receiver may have.
- Take enough time reflecting on what amends is, what amends isn't, false motives giving and amends.

Hurdles

- Their feelings may be centered on pain and anger.
  - Expect to stand under their feelings.
  - You will need to prepare for how they may react to you asking for forgiveness. If emotions are high, preparing some diffusing strategies may be needed. Seek counsel on such strategies from others more experienced at giving amends.
- Your higher power will be your strength through the amends-writing process and when you're giving the amends.
  - Dependence upon your higher power will be tested.
  - You are worth owning your defects and how they have caused pain to others. Remember that giving your amends and moving towards reconciliation is going to strengthen your recovery and your relationship with your higher power.

Answer the following questions with an honest heart.
Share the answers that impact you the most with others in recovery.

What does amends mean? What is amends NOT? What are false motives for making amends?

_____
_____
_____
_____
_____
_____
_____
_____

What do you feel when someone is dodgy, suspicious, or indirect towards you?

_____
_____
_____
_____
_____
_____
_____
_____

Name two positive changes you have seen in yourself since beginning recovery.

1. _____
_____

2. _____
_____

Name any examples of selfish motivation you've had when apologizing or making amends.

_____
_____
_____
_____
_____
_____

List any hopes you have about the outcome of making amends with those in your inventory.

_____
_____
_____
_____
_____
_____

List the self-care exercises you will need to practice while writing your amends. If you're not sure, reach out to others who've experienced the need for self-care while writing their amends.

_____
_____
_____
_____
_____

What would it sound like to offer amends to yourself for the decisions you've made in your addictions? Consider adding yourself to your list of persons to make amends to.

_____
_____
_____
_____
_____
_____
_____

No matter what the outcome is for giving amends, are you prepared? List possible outcomes you would need to be prepared for.

_____
_____
_____
_____
_____
_____
_____

What behavior changes have you demonstrated that will serve as evidence of your current state of recovery?

_____
_____
_____
_____
_____
_____
_____

How do you write an amends?

That question is rhetorical, but there is a great acronym for the structure for amends I heard from someone sharing their testimony about their amends. It is RUT - ABC. "When you're in a RUT, get out of it by following the ABC's."

R - Recognize the wrong

U - Understand the hurt

T - Take responsibility

A - Ask for forgiveness

BC – Behavior Change

Recognize the wrong: It is important that you start with and stay focused on your wrongs. This does not mean going into details about every specific instance of your wrongdoing. If the person brings up specific instances, which you have already acknowledged to yourself in inventory, then acknowledge that wrong to the person. Remember that it is not your job to control their emotions, and yes, they may experience a rollercoaster of emotions during the amends.

Understand the hurt: If the person interjects during this part of amends, give them the space to, and use that as an opportunity to understand their pain your wrong caused and is still causing for them.

R and U work together in amends. You may be going back and forth between the two. Give time and breathing room to the process of understanding the pain that your wrong caused them. So pause, breathe, and show them your sincerity, grief, and compassion. Give them eye contact here.

Take responsibility: Taking ownership of your wrong is a step towards being a healthy adult. We have been reacting and acting out of addiction for so long that we can often skip this step when forming intimacy by withholding, isolating, blaming, criticizing, and defending. It is crucial for the recipient to hear and feel a serious acknowledgement of responsibility.

Ask for forgiveness: This is what it says and nothing more. You are entering a vulnerable place where yes or no answers are both understandable. Prepare your heart for both. You should avoid pressuring the wounded person to forgive. This can be worded as a question or a statement.

Give pause after offering them a chance to forgive you.

Behavior Change: Speak to specific practices and habits you are practicing in your recovery. Express your praises on your road of recovery. Emphasize that you are still in process, taking things one day at a time, and will continue towards healing and recovery. This may also be a chance to stand under the wounded and their feelings from the amends. Asking them what they need from you – and then doing it, if it is a reasonable request from them – may be the next step for their healing.

In summary: this gives us a blueprint, like many of us need, to be able to structure amends. Realize that this is a process that healthy and recovered people make on a week-to-week/day-to-day basis when saying the wrong thing, getting defensive, or withholding intimacy.

Now, begin writing your amends for each person/group on your list. Use a separate document for each, or you may make it handwritten (especially if you plan to mail it or have it delivered).

Amends can be a step that takes a long time. That being said, it is important to begin planning out when, where, and how you will meet with those face-to-face amends recipients. In the amends tracker below, rewrite your list of people/groups, their location/number to contact, confirmation of amends offering being made, their response, and time/date/location of the planned amends.

Once you have an amends planned, it is important to rehearse and remind yourself of the reasons why you are giving amends. Who will you plan to rehearse with? Will you be open to feedback?

Remember not to give someone amends with the false expectation that they will reconcile with you. Their response to your amends is completely independent from the reasons why you are taking responsibility for your actions.

Amends Tracker/Planner/Reflection				
Person/ Organization	When	Location	Mode of Amends: Written/Letter Face-to-face Empty Chair	After Completed: My Feelings Their Reactions Outcome

Step 9 Summary

Congratulations on completing your ninth step.

- **Now, write a summary of what you have learned and experienced. Include:**

    - **Who were you able to deliver amends to? What was the outcome? Explain 1-2 of these experiences below.**
    - **How did your higher power help you through this process of amends?**
    - **How did others in recovery help you through this process of amends?**

_____
_____
_____
_____
_____
_____
_____
_____
_____
_____
_____
_____
_____
_____
_____
_____
_____
_____

THE 12 STEPS TO BECOMING WELL

Share your step summary with others in recovery. Be open to their feedback and what they have found in the importance of Step 9.

STEP 10

Step 10 - We continue to take personal inventory and, when in the wrong, we promptly admit it.

Goals

- From this point on, the end of this process is only the beginning.
  - The purpose of the 12 steps is to give you a new way to live your life. The primary way we do this in recovery is to have an open, honest, and ongoing personal inventory.
- Honesty is the goal, the main goal, the only goal in this step.

Expectations

- Your routines will begin to change.
  - Daily recovery work will begin evolving into fewer questions to answer in the step work and more reflection about everyday living.
- Immediately admitting you're wrong should be something you are practicing regularly already with weekly check-ins.
- Honesty becomes a way of living now, and going back to secrecy needs to be a thing of the past.

Hurdles

- Temptation will always be present in your life of recovery.
  - The truth is that we all slip and are not perfect.
  - Secrecy will be a temptation that can set you back, returning to steps 1, 2, and 3.
- Remember the cost and destruction from your addiction.
- This step is the launching point into lifelong healing and recovery. When the 12 steps are over, the fight isn't.
- You are worth a life of authentic relationships and freedom from your addictions.

Answer the following questions with an honest heart.
Share the answers that impact you the most with others in recovery.

You might want to photocopy the questions below so you can use them daily or weekly for ongoing 10th step inventory work.

Have you felt fear, anxiety, anger, defensiveness, or the desire to control this week? If so, do you know what's happening in your life that is at the heart of those emotions?

_____
_____
_____
_____
_____
_____
_____
_____
_____
_____
_____
_____

Have your character defects been evident to you or others today? And if so, how?

_____
_____
_____
_____
_____
_____
_____

Have any of your recent actions required amends or correction in the past week? And if so, how?

_____
_____
_____
_____
_____
_____
_____

Name an action you can take today to give yourself forgiveness and love in acceptance of your imperfections. Share this with someone in recovery who has completed their Step 10 and write down an action they've taken.

_____
_____
_____
_____
_____
_____

THE 12 STEPS TO BECOMING WELL

Step 10 is a practice. Acceptance of yourself, self-care, and self-forgiveness are a practice. Plan a time and space each day in which you can practice Step 10.

_____
_____
_____
_____
_____
_____
_____

Write or copy down a prayer you will use during your daily time to practice Step 10.

_____
_____
_____
_____
_____
_____
_____

How have you asked for help and received it today?

_____
_____
_____
_____
_____
_____
_____

What opportunities have you had today to help others?

Journaling exercise:

Over the next 2 weeks of your recovery, create a daily inventory of the issues and struggles that brought you to recovery, including but not exclusive to:

Dishonesty, Fear, Pride, Control, Defensiveness, Greed, Criticism, Blame, Impulsiveness, Impatience, Self-Critical, Perfectionism, Sarcasm, Manipulation, Sexual Addiction

Refer back to your Step 4 to remind yourself of what a daily inventory should look like.

Week One/Day One

THE 12 STEPS TO BECOMING WELL

Week One/Day Two

_____
_____
_____
_____
_____
_____
_____

Week One/Day Three

_____
_____
_____
_____
_____
_____
_____

Week One/Day Four

_____
_____
_____
_____
_____
_____
_____

FROM SEXUAL ADDICTION

Week One/Day Five

Week One/Day Six

Week One/Day Seven

THE 12 STEPS TO BECOMING WELL

Week Two/Day One

_____
_____
_____
_____
_____
_____
_____
_____

Week Two/Day Two

_____
_____
_____
_____
_____
_____
_____

Week Two/Day Three

_____
_____
_____
_____
_____
_____
_____

Week Two/Day Four

Week Two/Day Five

Week Two/Day Six

Week Two/Day Seven

Did you admit struggles/behaviors in your daily inventory? How do you plan to make amends for these daily inventories?

What tools do you have that will help you recognize your daily inventory?

When do you schedule your daily inventory? Why does this time work best for you?

_____
_____
_____
_____
_____
_____
_____

When will you be able to have an inventory check-in with your recovery partner?

_____
_____
_____
_____
_____
_____
_____

How will making a daily inventory aid your growth in recovery?

_____
_____
_____
_____
_____
_____

Why is it important to admit your wrongs quickly? Who benefits from this step in your recovery and why?

_____

Explain the last time you were caught off guard by an addiction that you thought was under control.

_____

Describe the encouragement and/or discouragement you feel about your recovery needing daily practices.

_____

Identify a weakness you have found strength from by relying upon your higher power. Then identify a weakness you are still trying to overcome by your own strength.

_____
_____
_____
_____
_____
_____
_____

Name the thoughts that tempt you regularly.

_____
_____
_____
_____
_____
_____
_____

In what ways, if any, are fear, guilt, or shame still affecting your ability to completely give or receive love?

_____
_____
_____
_____
_____
_____

THE 12 STEPS TO BECOMING WELL

What areas of your life do you still need to surrender and hand over to your higher power?

_____
_____
_____
_____
_____
_____
_____

List any fears, resentments, or pains affecting how you are responding to others. How are you responding to your higher power?

_____
_____
_____
_____
_____
_____
_____

Identify any areas of your life for which you doubt your higher power's will over your own.

_____
_____
_____
_____
_____

List any desires you have that overshadow consideration of others or wise counsel from others.

_____
_____
_____
_____
_____
_____
_____

Are there any hurts or traumas you still need to grieve? If so, please list them. Consider sharing them with a recovery partner and seeking advice for how to grieve properly.

_____
_____
_____
_____
_____
_____
_____

Are you needing to change any daily choices, behaviors, or habits that lead you to slip? List these changes and share them with a recovery partner. Give updates to your accountability partner and during weekly group.

_____
_____
_____
_____

Step 10 Summary

Congratulations on completing your tenth step.

- **Now, write a summary of what you have learned and experienced. Include:**

  - Any ongoing struggles/behaviors you are creating inventories for.
  - Your top 3 self-care exercises that help you in continuing recovery, with reasons why for each.

_____
_____
_____
_____
_____
_____
_____
_____
_____
_____
_____
_____
_____
_____
_____
_____
_____
_____
_____
_____
_____

FROM SEXUAL ADDICTION

Share your step summary with others in recovery. Be open to their feedback and what they have found in the importance of Step 10.

STEP 11

Step 11 - We seek to improve contact with our higher power through prayer and meditation, praying for knowledge of their will for our lives and the power to carry it out.

Goals

- We started with relying upon your higher power, and we end with relying upon your higher power.
- Creating ongoing habits, devotionals, meditations, and worship to your higher power will center your life on a will greater than your own.
- Continue to build upon your current walk with your higher power.
- Claim a life of peace with your higher power as your provider,
- not people, not materials, not your past coping mechanisms.

Expectations

- Your spiritual walk is only as good as how much effort you put into it.
  - This is your daily choice to put your higher power or idols first in your heart
- Surrendering your own will and seeking your higher power's will for your life is a practice, not a faucet or light switch.
- Whether in good times or desperate ones, you will continue to need to seek your higher power in order to seek ongoing recovery.

Hurdles

- **Feelings are not always something to be followed**

  - **Our own will gets in the way sometimes**
  - **Thinking you got it under control will lead to arrogance and pride**
  - **Boasting will lead to self-centeredness**

- **Remember how your higher power has helped you in this walk of recovery. Your higher power will be what leads you into a life of walking in humility and peace.**

Answer the following questions with an honest heart.
Share the answers that impact you the most with others in recovery.

List the things that you are grateful for.

_____
_____
_____
_____
_____
_____
_____
_____
_____
_____
_____
_____
_____
_____
_____
_____

FROM SEXUAL ADDICTION

What do your prayer and meditation practices currently look like?

Share your prayer and meditation practices with someone in recovery. Reflect with them on ways to improve or polish the practice to be more intimate with your higher power. Record details of that conversation here and come up with an action plan.

Are there any ways you have begun trying to take your will and control back from your higher power?

How will you begin surrendering your will back over to your higher power in these areas?

_____
_____
_____
_____
_____
_____
_____

How do you define prayer? How does your higher power define prayer?

_____
_____
_____
_____
_____
_____
_____

List out the overall benefits to your mental, physical, and relational health from daily prayer habits.

_____
_____
_____
_____
_____

How do you define meditation? How does your higher power define meditation?

_____
_____
_____
_____
_____
_____
_____

Do you harbor anger toward your higher power that results in avoidance of prayer and meditation? If so, reach out to others in recovery to help resolve your anger.

_____
_____
_____
_____
_____
_____
_____

What issues do you have relaxing due to other coping mechanisms you use? Including but not limited to caffeine, nicotine, adrenaline, or sugar.

_____
_____
_____
_____
_____
_____

THE 12 STEPS TO BECOMING WELL

Was there a time in your past when you misunderstood your higher power's will for you? If so, record those misunderstandings.

_____
_____
_____
_____
_____
_____
_____

What is the difference in how you now see your higher power's will for your life, as opposed to prior to entering recovery?

_____
_____
_____
_____
_____
_____
_____

Describe the importance of following your higher power's will for your life.

_____
_____
_____
_____
_____
_____

How has your higher power helped you carry out their will for your life?

_____
_____
_____
_____
_____
_____
_____
_____
_____
_____
_____

Create a future action plan for your prayer life. Note the best time, place, and reason for the necessity of daily prayer. Identify how you can practice prayer and meditation throughout the day.

_____
_____
_____
_____
_____
_____
_____
_____

THE 12 STEPS TO BECOMING WELL

Journaling your prayer and meditation time and contact with your higher power is meant to grow you spiritually.

Spend 3 days recording the prayers you make on a day-to-day basis. If it becomes something you would like to commit to on a long-term basis, do so.

Day One

_____
_____
_____
_____
_____
_____

Day Two

_____
_____
_____
_____
_____
_____

Day Three

_____
_____
_____
_____
_____
_____

Step 11 Summary

Congratulations on completing your eleventh step.

- **Now, write a summary of what you have learned about yourself in the space below.**
  Include:

  - **What you have learned about yourself, your addiction, and what you must choose to do in order to stay in recovery.**
  - **A summary of your future action plan for continuing prayer and meditation.**

THE 12 STEPS TO BECOMING WELL

Share your step summary with others in recovery. Be open to their feedback and what they have found in the importance of Step 11.

STEP 12

Step 12 - Having had a spiritual awakening from our experience through the steps, we seek to share with others and practice our principles in all our relationships.

Goals

- Pray for your higher power to use you, and to open doors to what may come next in your walk of recovery.
- Assess the season you're in.
- Stay connected with others in recovery even after commencing.
- Commencement means you aren't finished yet and will always be in the process.

Expectations

- You can develop purpose for your life in recovery.
  - Your higher power can use you and your story to impact the lives of others if you allow it.
  - Relationships with those seeking a better more free life from addictions will be unlike others, more vulnerable and loving
- Behaviors that you keep and take with you will be the evidence of real change

Hurdles

- Closing yourself off to your higher power or their purposes can feel tempting
    - Keeping your story to yourself
    - Thinking you got this now on your own
    - Resorting to old habits out of resentment from lost relationships
- Remember that your higher power wants a new life for you. You are worth lifelong healing and recovery.
- With the progress you've made, practice gratitude, and use any exercise up until this point whenever you need.
- Keep going, keep relying, keep believing that you are worth it!

Answer the following questions with an honest heart.
Share the answers that impact you the most with others in recovery.

How does serving others benefit my recovery?

_____
_____
_____
_____
_____
_____
_____
_____
_____
_____
_____
_____
_____

In what ways can I serve my recovery group?

Are my motives to help and serve others selfless and expecting nothing in return? What are my reasons when I help and serve others?

How will selflessly serving others progress my own recovery?

Create a plan, using your answers from above, for how you will serve others in and out of recovery after you are done with your 12th step. Include loved ones, family, friends, coworkers, employees, and the recovery group.

Person/Group/ Organization	Plan to Serve them by…

How are you spiritually different since entering recovery? Describe the difference in terms of your beliefs and feelings.

What is your current emotional state now that you are completing Step 12, and why?

What would you say to encourage others who are still struggling in their recovery and sobriety?

THE 12 STEPS TO BECOMING WELL

How will you plan to practice the twelve steps in your day-to-day life?

_____
_____
_____
_____
_____
_____
_____

Name specific ways your behavior has been an example of your recovery. At work? At home? With family?

_____
_____
_____
_____
_____
_____
_____

What service opportunities in your area, life, church, or career do you feel passionate about?

_____
_____
_____
_____
_____

What steps were most influential in your recovery and why?

What is most important to you as you end the 12-step process?

Step 12 Summary

Congratulations on completing your twelfth step.

- **Now, write a summary of what you have learned about yourself in the space below. Include:**

  - **Encouragement toward other participants for the full completion of the twelve steps.**
  - **A summary of your action plan to serve others (in any area of your life).**

- **Describe why two of the steps (your choice) were most influential to you.**

_____
_____
_____
_____
_____
_____
_____
_____
_____
_____
_____
_____
_____
_____
_____
_____
_____
_____
_____
_____

Share your step summary with others in recovery. Be open to their feedback and what they have found in the importance of Step 12.

Parting Words

In closing, I would like to thank you for reading this book. We hope that it was helpful to you. While I know the road is long and tough to navigate, I encourage you to keep pressing on. As Winston Churchill once said, *"If you are going through hell, keep going."* If you do the work, don't give in, and seek help along the way, I know you will find your way out of the painful circumstances in which you have found yourself. We wish you healing, comfort, peace, and wholeness in your recovery journey.

Addendum

Feeling Wheel

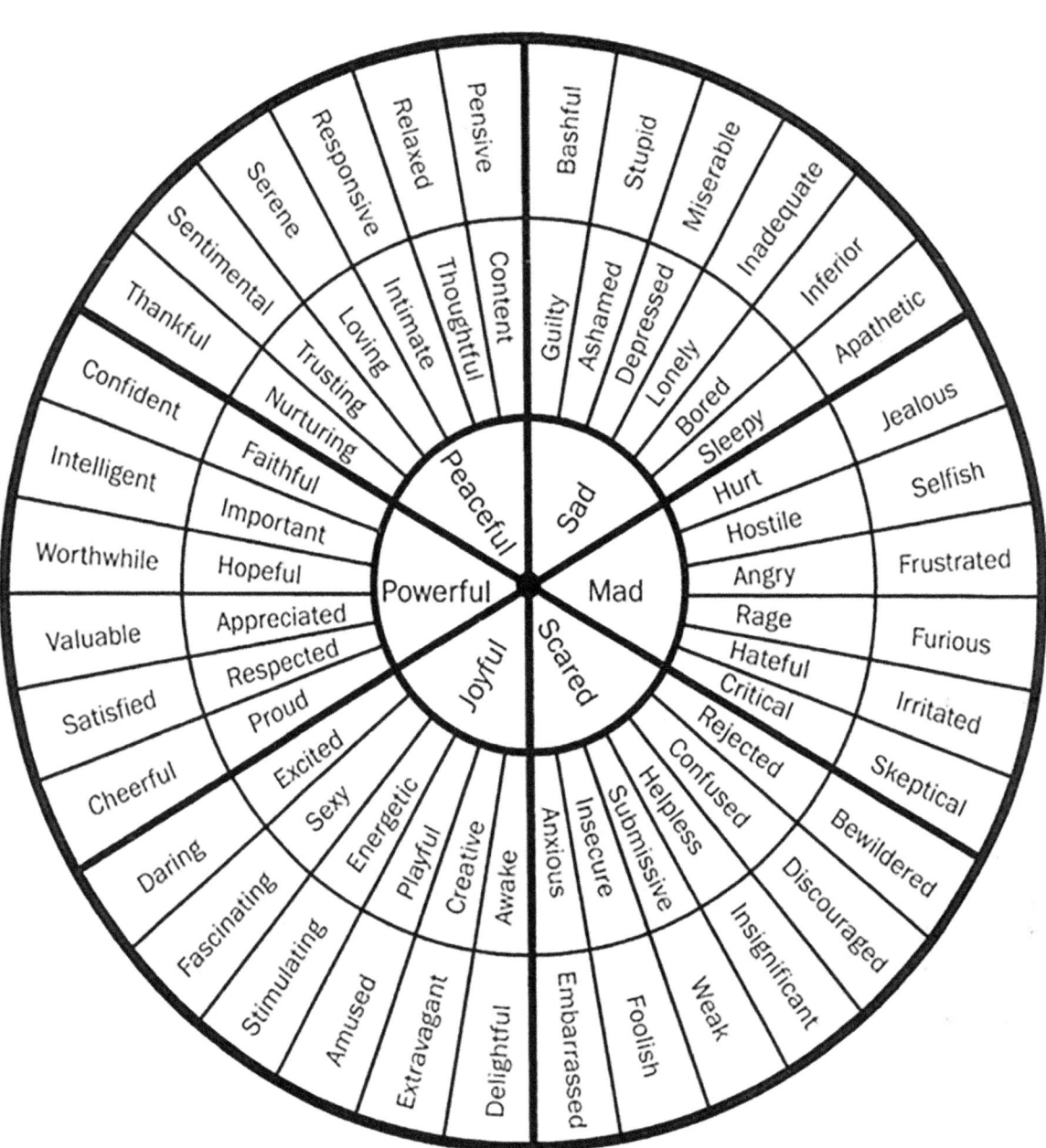

The Twelve Steps for Sexual Addiction

1. We admitted we were powerless over lust and that our lives had become unmanageable

2. We came to believe that a power greater than ourselves could restore us to sanity.

3. We made a decision to turn our will and lives over to the care of our higher power as we understand them.

4. We made a searching and fearless moral inventory of ourselves.

5. We admitted to our higher power, to ourselves, and to others the exact nature of our wrongs.

6. We were entirely ready to have our higher power remove all these defects of character.

7. We humbly asked our higher power to remove our struggle.

8. We made a list of all people we had harmed, and we became willing to make amends with them all.

9. We made direct amends to whomever possible, except when to do so would injure them or others.

10. We continue to take personal inventory and, when in the wrong, we promptly admit it.

11. We seek through prayer and meditation to improve contact with our higher power, praying for knowledge of their will for our lives and the strength to carry it out.

12. Having had a spiritual awakening from our experience through the steps, we seek to share with others and practice our principles in all our relationships.

The Twelve Steps of AA (Alcoholics Anonymous)

1. We admitted we were powerless over alcohol — that our lives had become unmanageable.

2. Came to believe that a power greater than ourselves could restore us to sanity.

3. Made a decision to turn our will and our lives over to the care of our higher power as we understood them.

4. Made a searching and fearless moral inventory of ourselves.

5. Admitted to our higher power, to ourselves, and to another human being the exact nature of our wrongs.

6. Were entirely ready to have our higher power remove all these defects of character.

7. Humbly asked our higher power to remove our shortcomings.

8. Made a list of all persons we had harmed, and became willing to make amends to them all.

9. Made direct amends to such people wherever possible, except when to do so would injure them or others.

10. Continued to take personal inventory and when we were wrong promptly admitted it.

11. Sought through prayer and meditation to improve our conscious contact with our higher power as we understood them, praying only for knowledge of their will for us and the power to carry that out.

12. Having had a spiritual awakening as the result of these Steps, we tried to carry this message to alcoholics, and to practice these principles in all our affairs.

Recovery and 12 Step Prayers

Third Step Prayer (Page 63, AA Big Book)

God, I offer myself to Thee — to build with me and to do with me as Thou wilt. Relieve me of the bondage of self, that I may better do Thy will. Take away my difficulties, that victory over them may bear witness to those I would help of Thy Power, Thy Love, and Thy Way of life. May I do Thy will always!

Fourth Step Prayer (Page 67, AA Big Book)

This is a sick man. How can I be helpful to him? God, save me from being angry. Thy will be done.

Seventh Step Prayer (Page 76, AA Big Book)

My Creator, I am now willing that you should have all of me, good & bad. I pray that you now remove from me every single defect of character that stands in the way of my usefulness to you & my fellows. Grant me strength, as I go from here to do Your bidding. Amen.

Eighth Step Prayer (Page 76, AA Big Book)

Faith without works is dead.

Tenth Step Prayer (Page 85, AA Big Book)

How can I serve Thee? Thy will (not mine) be done.

Eleventh Step Prayer (Twelve Steps and Twelve Traditions, p. 99)

Lord, make me a channel of Thy peace – that where there is hatred, I may bring love – that where there is wrong, I may bring the spirit of forgiveness – that where there is discord, I may bring harmony – that where there is error, I may bring truth--that where there is doubt, I may bring faith--that where there is despair, I may bring hope – that where there are shadows, I may bring light – that where there is sadness, I may bring joy. Lord, grant that I may seek to comfort rather than to be comforted – to understand, than to be understood – to love, than to be loved. For it is by self-forgetting that one finds. It is by forgiving that one is forgiven. It is by dying that one awakens to eternal life. Amen

Serenity Prayer (Reinhold Niebuhr)

God, grant me the serenity to accept the things I cannot change,
The courage to change the things I can,
And the wisdom to know the difference.

SA/PA Lapse and Relapse Worksheet

Instructions: Answer the following questions to help you figure out what led to you acting out with pornography or inappropriate sexual behavior.

On a separate piece of paper:

- **Describe the main reason you used pornography or behaved in a sexually inappropriate way.**

- **Describe the inner thoughts and feelings that triggered your need or desire to use pornography or act out sexually.**

- **Describe any external circumstances that triggered your need or desire to use pornography or act out sexually.**

- **Think back to when this started. Describe the first decision you made (or remember making) that started the lapse or relapse process.**

Resources

Men's Becoming Well Workgroups

Some guys have been in groups before; others have not. If you're committed to recovery from Sexual Addiction, Intimacy Avoidance, or Infidelity and are committed to rebuilding trust in your marriage, then our Men's Becoming Well Workgroups will be a good fit for you. Our men's groups focus on building and maintaining integrity, restoring intimacy in relationships, and rebuilding trust. They concentrate on two things: how to stop acting out and be accountable for the behavior that is breaking trust in the relationship, and how to develop the character and empathy it will take to support the relationship moving forward. And unlike many recovery groups out there, our guys are both finding sobriety and maintaining it.

Our groups are led by trained facilitators who have walked through many of these issues themselves, know how to stay sober, and know how to win in their relationship. The groups are small in size (no more than 8 people) so that each person can get the attention they need to address specific issues.

Each week, participants will hear teaching from a trained professional and receive assignments and exercises that facilitate recovery for both themselves and their relationships. Participants will also have access to an online education portal, videos that explain the concepts talked about during group, and tutorials on how to work exercises and complete assignments.

Another thing that makes our groups different is that we welcome input from the wounded partners. Most programs exclude the partner, expecting that they stay in a relationship and take their partner's word for it that they're doing the work. When we hear from partners about past experiences, they often complain that nothing was shared with them, and they didn't even know what was going on most of the time.

Although we want to stress that the men need to own and work through their own recovery, and no partner can do that for them, we assign exercises to include the partner in rebuilding the relationship. Additionally, we offer a free monthly video conference call in which we update partners on what the guys will be working on that month and allow them to ask questions. Those meetings are typically led by Matt and Laura Burton personally.

Join a Men's Becoming Well workgroup today

www.MyBecomingWell.com

Guys Group Intensives

Aka Men's Becoming Well Bootcamps

Are you a guy or married to a guy who's stuck or in a downward spiral, relationally or in your individual recovery, unable to do what's needed/necessary to heal the shattered trust in your relationship?

Our Guys Group Intensives focus on moving guys from playing to not lose to playing to win. Moving from working your relational and individual recovery as a way to avoid losing the relationship to doing it to win - win your partner's heart and trust back, and win back your life and your integrity.

These unique intensives are 3 days long and address issues related to intimacy avoidance, sexual or pornography addiction, and infidelity. Bootcamps are limited to 12 participants at a time.

These intensives are especially helpful to anyone whose partner is not ready to participate in a recovery program, guys who are stuck, or guys new to recovery who want to get off to a great start. Participants have the added bonus of getting to know other men who can provide support and accountability throughout the recovery process.

This is great option for anyone wanting to accelerate the healing process, because intensives take 4-6 months' worth of session work and condense it into 3 days. You will receive an assessment of your unique issues, 7-8 hours per day of instruction, exercises and tools to help you move forward, and a personalized recovery plan for yourself and/or your relationship. We provide you a shame-free environment to address your specific issues.

We need you to learn how to stand "Shoulder to Shoulder with your partner in their pain." We spend a lot of time in the Guys Group Intensives showing you, teaching you, and having you practice how to do that. It makes many times the difference along with embracing your own recovery on whether the relationship is able to find long-term healing and be saved.

Our intensive center in located in beautiful, sunny Tucson, Arizona.
Learn more or sign up for a Guys Group Intensive today

www.MyBecomingWell.com

Private Couple's Intensive

Moving couples from "Shattered to Strong"

Couples that attend Our One-on-One Private Couple's Intensives say it helps couples understand and begin or advance the long journey of healing from the immediate and ongoing impacts of porn addiction, sexual addiction, infidelity &/or Intimacy avoidance - for both the Wounding and Wounded partner. We are able to take the time to deep-dive into what's specifically destroying the trust, individually and as a couple, and find the recovery you're desperately trying to either rediscover or discover for the first time.

For many couples, this intensive is their last stop before divorce court or a decision to stay permanent roommates. Couple after couple says that their time at the intensive allowed them to identify and begin the process of healing the hurt and devastation, as well as giving them a new relational system, as their current one just doesn't work for many reasons.

If you choose a Private Couple's Intensive, we will work with you to identify your specific needs to make sure your concerns are fully addressed in a private setting. Our Private Couple's Intensives are 3 days in length and will address both people in the relationship individually as well as the relationship itself.

Like the Guys Group Intensive, our Private Couple's Intensive is a great option for anyone wanting to accelerate the healing process, because intensives take 4-6 months' worth of session work and condense it into 3 days. You will receive an assessment of your unique issues, 7-8 hours per day of instruction, exercises and tools to help you move forward, and a personalized recovery plan for yourself and/or your relationship. We provide you a shame-free environment to address your specific issues.

And, if you choose a Private Couple's Intensive, we want you to know that partners are always treated with respect, compassion, and validation for the pain that their partner's issues have caused them. As a partner, you will never be blamed or asked to take any responsibility for your partner's choices. Also, if desired, we have full disclosure and polygraph services available.

Learn more or sign up for a Private Couple's Intensive today

www.MyBecomingWell.com

Books and Courses

Moving Couples from Shattered to Strong

REBUILDING TRUST

A Couple's Guide to Healing After Betrayal

MATT BURTON
LAURA BURTON

www.MyBecomingWell.com

Books and Courses

Moving Couples from Shattered to Strong

REBUILDING TRUST  FOR CHRISTIANS

A Couple's Guide to Healing After Betrayal

MATT BURTON
LAURA BURTON

www.MyBecomingWell.com

Books and Courses

Moving Partners from Shattered to Strong

Mending After Betrayal

BOOK AND WORKBOOK

LAURA BURTON

www.MyBecomingWell.com

Books and Courses

Moving Partners from Shattered to Strong

Mending After Betrayal

BOOK AND WORKBOOK FOR CHRISTIANS

LAURA BURTON

www.MyBecomingWell.com

Books and Courses

www.MyBecomingWell.com

Books and Courses

www.MyBecomingWell.com

Books and Courses

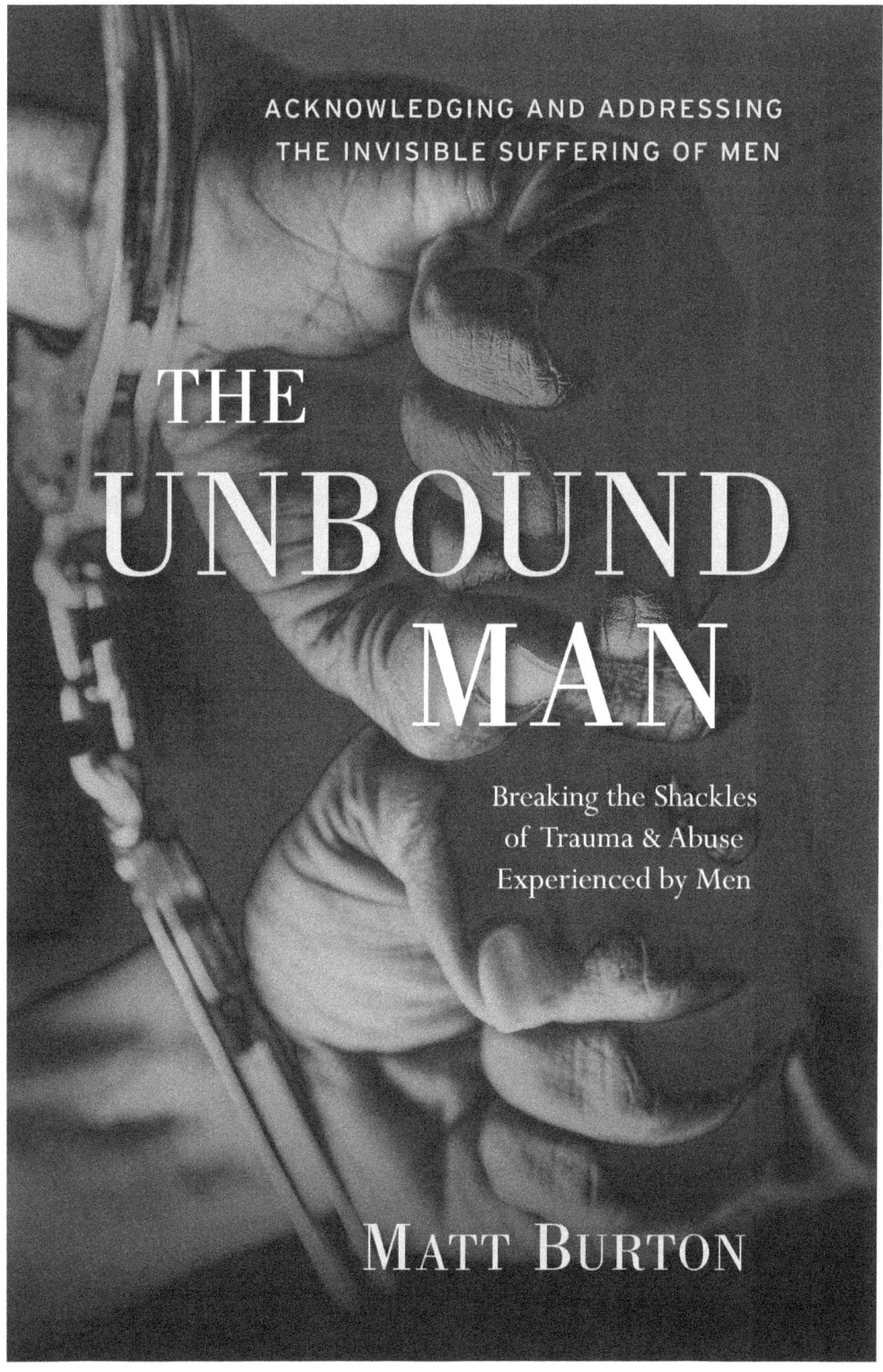

www.MyBecomingWell.com

Books and Courses

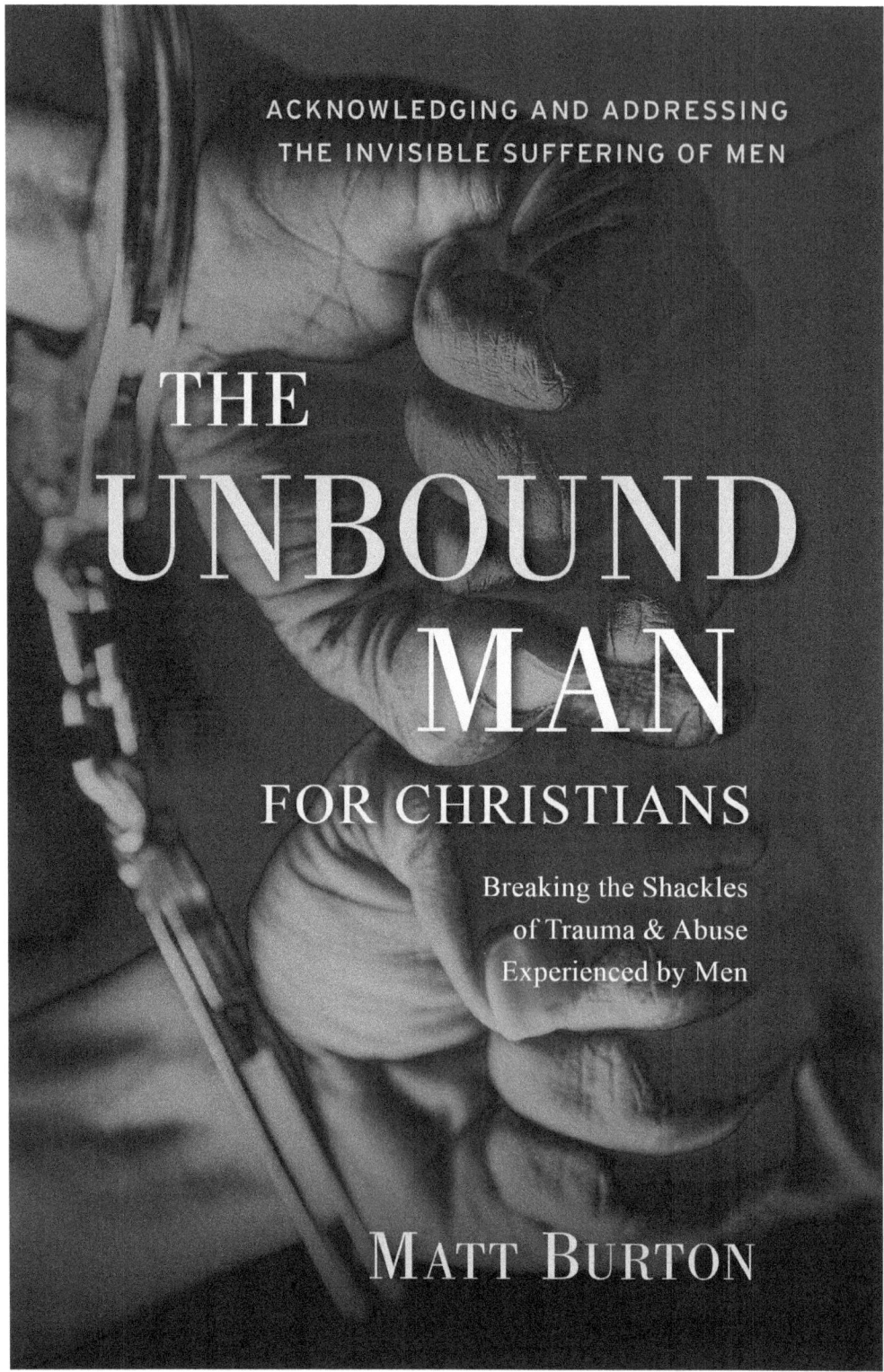

www.MyBecomingWell.com

Books and Courses

www.MyBecomingWell.com

Connect with Us

 www.facebook.com/mybecomingwell

 Becoming Well (@mybecomingwell)

 Becoming Well (@mybecomingwell)

 www.mybecomingwell.com

 info@mybecomingwell.com

 520-355-5322

www.ingramcontent.com/pod-product-compliance
Lightning Source LLC
LaVergne TN
LVHW081456060526
838201LV00057BA/3056